PLAY THE PART

TRAIN DRIVER

Written by Liz Gogerly

Photographs by Chris Fairclough

Published in 2014 by Wayland

Copyright © Wayland 2014

Wayland
338 Euston Road
London NW1 3BH

Wayland Australia
Level 17/207 Kent Street
Sydney, NSW 2000

Editors: Paul Humphrey, James Nixon
Series design: D. R. ink
Design: Ian Winton
Model maker: Tom Humphrey
Commissioned photography: Chris Fairclough
Picture credits: First Capital Connect: pp. 5, 7 top; Northern Rail: pp. 6, 8 top; Shutterstock: pp. 4 top (hfng),
4 bottom (Kenneth Sponsler), 14 top (Bartlomiej Magierowski); Virgin Trains: pp. 12 top, 14 bottom.

British Library Cataloguing in Publication Data
Gogerly, Liz.
   Train driver. -- (Play the part)
   1. Train Drivers--Juvenile literature. 2. Train Drivers--
   Juvenile drama. 3. Role playing--Juvenile literature.
   I. Title II. Series
   388.3'22-dc22

ISBN 978 0 7502 8873 6

First published in 2011

Printed in China

Wayland is a division of
Hachette Children's Books,
an Hachette UK Company

www.hachette.co.uk

The author, packager and publisher
would like to thank Davigdor Infants'
School, Hove for their help and
participation in this book.

Contents

What is a train driver?

Train drivers work on the railways. They can drive passenger trains (right) or freight trains (below).

Passenger trains have **coaches** for carrying people to different **destinations**. Freight trains have **wagons** for carrying **cargo** from one place to another.

At the front of all trains there is an engine that pulls the coaches and wagons along. Train drivers sit in the **driver's cabin** at the front of the train. They control when the train starts and stops and the speed at which the train travels. It's the train driver's job to make sure everybody on the train is safe.

A train driver's day

There is more to being a train driver than just driving the trains. At the start of every journey they make safety checks on the train. At the end of each trip they write a report about what happened on the journey.

Train drivers go on railway journeys to many different places. They stop at stations along the way.

Make your own railway poster

Think of an exciting railway journey and make a railway poster advertising a trip there. It could be to a seaside town like Salty By Sea on pages 16–17.

You will need:

- ★ A sheet of white paper
- ★ Magazines
- ★ Felt-tip pens
- ★ Paints
- ★ Glue
- ★ Scissors

1 Take some paper and write the name of a place in large capital letters e.g. SALTY BY SEA.

2 Write something exciting about the place, such as: 'HAVE FUN IN THE SUN!' or 'SO MUCH TO SEE'!

3 Add something about train travel like: 'TAKE THE TRAIN TODAY!' or 'THE RAILWAY IS THE BEST WAY'.

4 Paint your own picture of the place or cut out pictures from a magazine and glue them onto the poster.

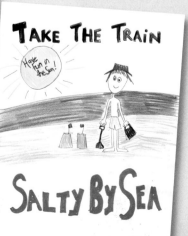

Dress like a train driver

Train drivers, **conductors** and railway station staff usually wear a uniform. Each rail company has its own uniform with its name and **logo** on it. Most drivers wear dark-coloured trousers and matching jackets. Sometimes they wear a cap.

You can buy a train driver costume from the shops. Otherwise make your own uniform from matching trousers and jacket. You could make a badge with your own railway company name and logo on it, and stick it to the jacket.

Name:
Zac Brown

WHIZZ WEST NETWORK

Go FAST TRAINS →

NAME: SALLY JONES

In the role plays in this book there are plenty of train passengers. They will usually be wearing everyday clothes. You could also collect real cases and bags for your passengers.

The conductor

On many passenger trains there are conductors. They move along the train checking passengers' tickets. They make sure that people have the correct ticket for the journey. Sometimes they take **fares** and give out tickets.

Make your own ticket machine

Conductors carry a ticket machine that prints tickets. This is how you make your own ticket machine. You could also make your own tickets to go with the machine.

You will need:
- ★ A cardboard shoebox
- ★ A sheet of thin white card
- ★ Silver paint
- ★ Black paint
- ★ Small round stickers
- ★ 2 bottle tops
- ★ White paper
- ★ A long strip of thin black card
- ★ A black felt-tip pen
- ★ Glue
- ★ Sticky tape
- ★ Scissors

1 Glue the lid of the shoebox to the box.

2 Paint the sides of the box silver and the top black.

3 Cut out a rectangle of white card to make a screen for the ticket machine. Write '£ 0.00' on the screen and glue it to the side of the box.

4 Stick the small round stickers next to the screen and write numbers 0 to 9 on the stickers.

5 Cut out a small rectangle of white paper and stick it on top of a bottle top. Write 'ISSUE TICKET' on top of the paper.

6 Stick the bottle tops next to the small round stickers on the front of the machine.

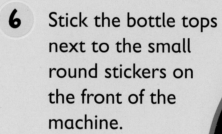

7 To make a strap for the ticket machine stick one end of the black card to one side of the ticket machine using sticky tape. Repeat on the other side.

In the driver's seat

Train drivers sit in the driver's cabin. Inside the driver's cabin there is a control panel. This has buttons, **levers**, **dials** and a computer screen to help the driver control the train.

Train drivers make **announcements** to the passengers using a **public address system**. They tell the passengers when the train is approaching a station or if there is an emergency.

Make your own train driver's control panel

This is how you make a control panel with a public address system.

You will need:

★ 2 large cereal boxes
★ Silver paint
★ Black paint
★ 2 wooden spoons
★ 2 sheets of light green card
★ 4 bottle tops
★ A plastic drinking cup
★ String
★ Scissors
★ Glue
★ Pen
★ Sticky tape

1   Cut out two long slots measuring about 1 cm wide and 10 cm long from the front of one of the cereal boxes.

2   Glue the two cereal boxes together and paint with silver paint.

3   To make a computer screen, cut a rectangle of green card. Write 'JOURNEY PLANNER' on the screen. Glue the screen to the front of the second cereal box.

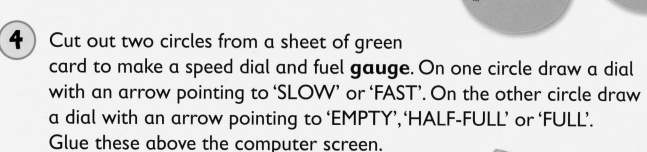

4   Cut out two circles from a sheet of green card to make a speed dial and fuel **gauge**. On one circle draw a dial with an arrow pointing to 'SLOW' or 'FAST'. On the other circle draw a dial with an arrow pointing to 'EMPTY', 'HALF-FULL' or 'FULL'. Glue these above the computer screen.

5   Stick the bottle tops next to the slots on the first cereal box to make buttons.

6   To make the public address system, paint the drinking cup with silver paint. Attach a piece of string from the cup to the first cereal box using sticky tape.

7   Use the wooden spoons to make levers for the control panel. Paint the ends of the spoons with black paint and then paint the rest of the spoons with silver paint. Place the spoons in the slots you made earlier.

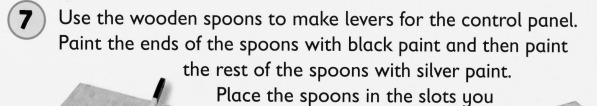

All aboard!

Passenger trains have coaches for people to sit in. Inside each coach there are seats, tables and luggage racks.

Some trains also have a **buffet car** where food and drink is served.

Set up your own passenger train

To make the coach, arrange four chairs around one table for the passengers. Place the table in front of a window and put luggage behind the chairs.

You can decorate the walls of the coach with posters and maps. To make the driver's cab, arrange a chair behind a table and put it in front of the coach.

Place the train driver's control panel on the table. Your train is ready to depart!

15

You have set the scene and made some props. Now you can begin to play the part of a train driver in these role plays.

The Seaside Express

Play the parts of the train driver and passengers making a rail trip to the seaside. The passengers can wear summer clothes and have buckets, spades and swimming gear with them.

 JACK: Are we there yet?

 ROSE: No! It takes one hour to get there.

 TRAIN DRIVER: *(speaks into the public address system)* We are now approaching Green Hill station. *(train stops at the station then sets off again)*

 SOPHIE: Salty By Sea is the next stop.

 JACK: Great! I can't wait to get to the beach. *(The train driver puts on the brakes and makes an emergency stop.)*

 ROSE: Oh dear! What's happening?

SOPHIE: Oh no, the train is stopping!

TRAIN DRIVER: *(speaks into the public address system)* Ladies and gentlemen, we have had to make an emergency stop. There is no need to panic.

 JACK: Oh bother! We'll never get to the beach now…

WHAT HAPPENS NEXT?

You can decide what happens next in this scene. Below are some fun ideas that you could try acting out using your own words. Then have a go at making up your own scenes.

1 The train driver says that there was something on the rails so he had to stop. Nobody is injured and the train carries on to the seaside. Everyone gets off the train for a fun day at the beach.

2 The train driver tells the passengers that the railway lines are broken. The train driver has to take a different route to the seaside.

3 The train driver says that somebody pressed the **emergency button** on the train by accident.

Tickets please!

In this scene a conductor checks the tickets of the passengers on the train. You can use the ticket machine you made on pages 10–11.

 CONDUCTOR: *(enters coach)* Good morning ladies and gentlemen. Tickets please!

 MR GREEN: I'm sure I put the tickets in my pocket?

(looks in his pocket)

 MRS GREEN: I thought I put them in my bag.

(looks in her handbag)

MILLIE: What happens if we can't find the tickets?

CONDUCTOR: Well, if you've lost them, you will have to buy new tickets.

MILLIE and JOE: What? *(look worried)* We're going on holiday.

CONDUCTOR: I'm sure it's all going to be OK!

WHAT HAPPENS NEXT?

You can decide what happens next in this scene. Below are some fun ideas that you could try acting out using your own words. Then have a go at making up your own scenes.

1 Mrs Green finds the tickets in her bag. Everyone has a good laugh.

2 Mr Green remembers he left the tickets in the kitchen at home. The ticket inspector issues the family with new tickets.

3 Mr Green left the tickets and his wallet at home. Mrs Green hasn't got enough money with her to pay the full fare. The family all have to get off the train at the next station.

Snow on the tracks

Play the parts of the train driver, conductor and passengers in this scene. Find out what happens when snow begins to fall. You will need a white sheet for the snow and spades for digging.

 TRAIN DRIVER: *(speaks into the public address system)* Good morning. Welcome all passengers on board this North Hills Rail train to Aberdoolie. I wish you all a safe and pleasant journey.

 JOSH: This should be a fun trip.

 JOSH'S MOTHER: Yes, I'm going to relax and look out the window.

 JOSH: I'm going to have a snack.

KATE: It looks like it's going to snow.

 KATE'S DAD: I'm sure it will be fine.

 CONDUCTOR: *(walks up to Kate's table)* Tickets please, Sir!

 KATE'S DAD: *(shows tickets to conductor)* How long will it take to get there?

 CONDUCTOR: *(looks at ticket)* About three hours, Sir.

JOSH: *(points out of window)* Oh, it is snowing.

KATE: Look Dad, the fields are all white.

(continued over page)

21

Snow on the tracks (continued)

(The snow falls thick and fast and the train stops.)

 TRAIN DRIVER: Ladies and gentlemen, the train is stuck in a **snowdrift**. We cannot move.

 JOSH: Oh no!

 KATE: What will we do?

 CONDUCTOR: Don't panic.

 TRAIN DRIVER: *(enters the coach)* Sorry! We need some help to dig us out of the snowdrift. Please can some of you get off the train and help?

(The train driver and some of the passengers get off the train. They grab spades and planks of wood and begin digging the train out of the snow.)

TRAIN DRIVER: Fantastic work! I think the train will be able to move now.

(*Everyone gets back on the train, the passengers sit down and the train driver gets back in the driver's cabin.*)

 TRAIN DRIVER: (*speaks into the public address system*) Thank you ladies and gentlemen for all your help. Next stop Aberdoolie…

WHAT HAPPENS NEXT?

You can decide what happens next in this scene. Below are some fun ideas that you could try acting out using your own words. Then have a go at making up your own scenes.

1   The train driver tries to the start the train but it has broken down. The passengers wait for hours to be rescued.

2   The train starts up and makes its way slowly through the snow. The passengers enjoy free cups of hot chocolate and cake from the buffet car!

3   The train travels a few kilometres but then gets stuck again. The passengers have to get off the train in the middle of nowhere.

GLOSSARY

announcement A spoken message by the train driver to the passengers on a train.

buffet car A coach on a train where food is served.

cargo Goods that are carried on board a train, ship or plane.

coach A carriage on a train holding passengers.

conductor A person who sells tickets on a train.

destination The place where a train journey ends or where the train stops along the route.

dial An instrument which has a face like a clock with pointers to show measurements, such as speed or how much fuel there is.

driver's cabin The room at the front of a train engine where the train driver sits and controls the train.

emergency button A button that can be pressed to warn the train driver that there is an emergency and that they should stop the train immediately.

emergency stop When the train stops suddenly because of an emergency.

fare The amount of money it costs to buy a train ticket.

gauge A device that measures and displays the amount or level of something, such as fuel in a tank.

lever A bar which can be pulled up and down to move different parts of the train.

logo The symbol for a company.

public address system A machine with a microphone and speakers that is used for delivering spoken messages.

snowdrift A pile of deep snow that has been blown there by the wind.

wagon A section of a train that carries heavy goods.

INDEX